RUKMI, THE SON OF KING BHEESHMAKA OF VIDARBHA, CAME HOME FROM MATHURA, BURSTING WITH NEWS.

AS THE MEMBERS OF THE ROYAL HOUSEHOLD SURROUNDED HIM—

KRISHNA, THE COWHERD FROM VRINDAVAN, HAS SLAIN KAMSA.

* IT WAS FORETOLD THAT VISHNU, REBORN AS THE EIGHTH SON OF DEVAKI, WOULD SLAY KAMSA.

...DON'T FORGET HE DEPOSED HIS OWN FATHER AND USURPED THE THRONE.
I SUPPOSE KRISHNA WILL NOW BECOME THE KING.

NO! HE REFUSED THE CROWN. HE INSISTED THAT UGRASENA BE REINSTATED.
HE REFUSED THE CROWN!

YES! BUT KING UGRASENA AND THE NOBLES HAVE REQUESTED, NAY, INSISTED THAT HE REMAIN IN MATHURA AND...
WHO WOULDN'T! DID HE AGREE?

RUKMI IGNORED HER AND CONTINUED TO SPEAK TO BHEESHMAKA.
HE HAS AGREED TO STAY FOR A WHILE – TO LEARN THE SCRIPTURES AND THE PRINCELY ARTS.
WHAT ABOUT JARASANDHA? HOW DID HE REACT?

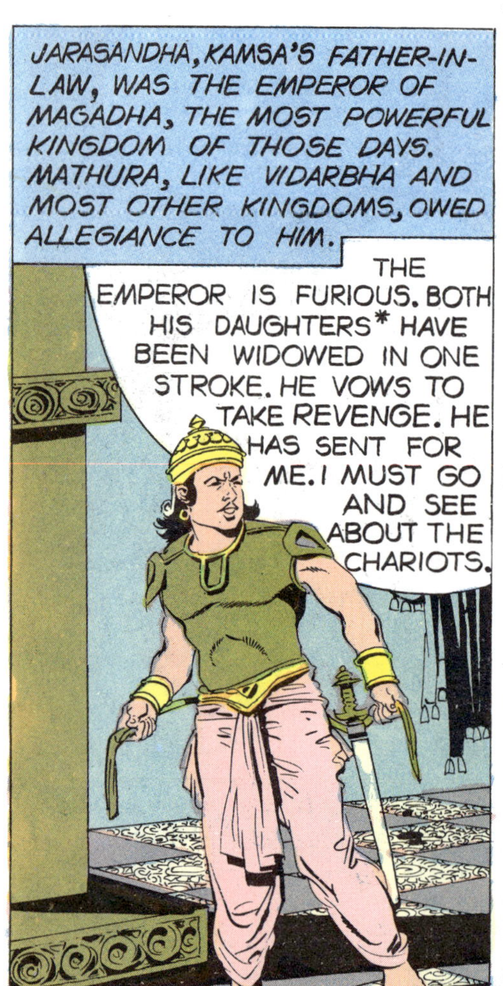

*KAMSA'S WIVES.

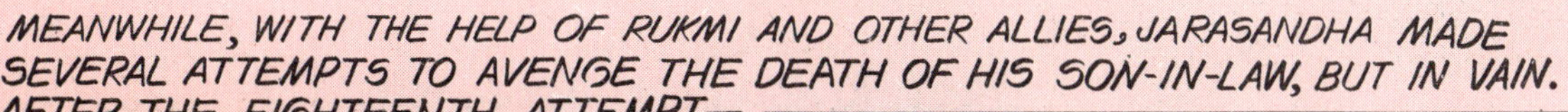

MEANWHILE, WITH THE HELP OF RUKMI AND OTHER ALLIES, JARASANDHA MADE SEVERAL ATTEMPTS TO AVENGE THE DEATH OF HIS SON-IN-LAW, BUT IN VAIN. AFTER THE EIGHTEENTH ATTEMPT—
THE VILE YADAVA AND HIS BROTHER HAVE DODGED US AGAIN. WE WILL HAVE TO BIDE OUR TIME. LET MY FRIENDS RETURN TO THEIR CAPITALS FOR THE PRESENT.

AT DWARAKA, KRISHNA'S INACCESSIBLE ISLAND CITY—
OUR SPIES SAY THAT JARASANDHA HAS DECIDED TO LIE LOW FOR A WHILE.

BALARAMA LOOKED AT KRISHNA WITH A MERRY TWINKLE IN HIS EYE.
NOW YOU'LL HAVE ALL THE LEISURE TO DREAM OF THE BEAUTIFUL PRINCESS OF VIDARBHA - THE MOST SOUGHT-AFTER PRINCESS ON EARTH.

AH, BALARAMA! MY MIND IS SET ON MARRYING HER. BUT HER FATHER IS A VASSAL OF JARASANDHA AND HER BROTHER, RUKMI, HIS STAUNCH ALLY.
BUT IT IS RUMOURED THAT BHEESHMAKA AND HIS WIFE SECRETLY HOPE THAT YOU WILL WIN RUKMINI.

MEANWHILE, AT VIDARBHA, IN THE GARDEN OF BHEESMAKA'S PALACE, RUKMINI TOO WAS LOST IN DREAMS OF THE YADAVA HERO WHO HAD WON HER HEART.
EVEN THE MIGHTY EMPEROR WITH ALL HIS ALLIES HAS NOT BEEN ABLE TO VANQUISH HIM. HE AND ONLY HE SHALL BE MY LORD.

SUDDENLY SHE HEARD VOICES.
MY FATHER! RUKMI! THEY'RE COMING THIS WAY.

THEY WERE DISCUSSING HER MARRIAGE.
YOUR MOTHER AND I HAVE DECIDED TO GIVE HER TO KRISHNA.
HOW FORTUNATE AM I!

HOW COULD YOU, FATHER? DON'T FORGET, HE MURDERED MY DEAR FRIEND, THE EMPEROR'S SON-IN-LAW. SURELY, WE CANNOT AFFORD TO DISPLEASE THE MIGHTY EMPEROR.
PLEASE RUKMI! DON'T MAKE HIM CHANGE HIS MIND!

BHEESHMAKA WAS SILENT FOR A WHILE. THEN—
BUT WE CANNOT THINK OF A MORE SUITABLE HUSBAND FOR HER. AFTER ALL JARASANDHA HAS NOT YET BEEN ABLE TO AVENGE KAMSA'S DEATH...
BUT HE CERTAINLY WILL. IT IS ONLY A MATTER OF TIME.

THEN WHOM DO YOU SUGGEST?
THE EMPEROR'S FAVOURITE AND MY FRIEND — SHISHUPALA, THE CROWN PRINCE OF CHEDI. HE IS ENAMOURED OF RUKMINI.

THAT JACKAL! NEVER! I SHALL NEVER MARRY HIM. O RUKMI, HOW COULD YOU SELL YOUR OWN SISTER TO WIN THE EMPEROR'S FAVOUR? DON'T AGREE, FATHER, PLEASE DON'T AGREE!

BUT BHEESHMAKA INVARIABLY PERMITTED HIS ELDEST SON TO MAKE ALL MAJOR DECISIONS, EVEN IF THEY DID NOT COINCIDE WITH HIS OWN WISHES. HE HEAVED A SIGH.
ALL RIGHT, RUKMI. DO AS YOU WILL.
THEN I SHALL SEND A FORMAL PROPOSAL TO CHEDI AND INVITE SHISHUPALA TO COME AND MARRY RUKMINI.

THEY WALKED AWAY, LITTLE KNOWING THAT RUKMINI HAD OVERHEARD EVERY WORD OF THEIR CONVERSATION.
SO THEY DON'T EVEN PLAN TO HOLD A SWAYAMWARA. TO WHOM SHALL I SPEAK? WHAT SHALL I DO?

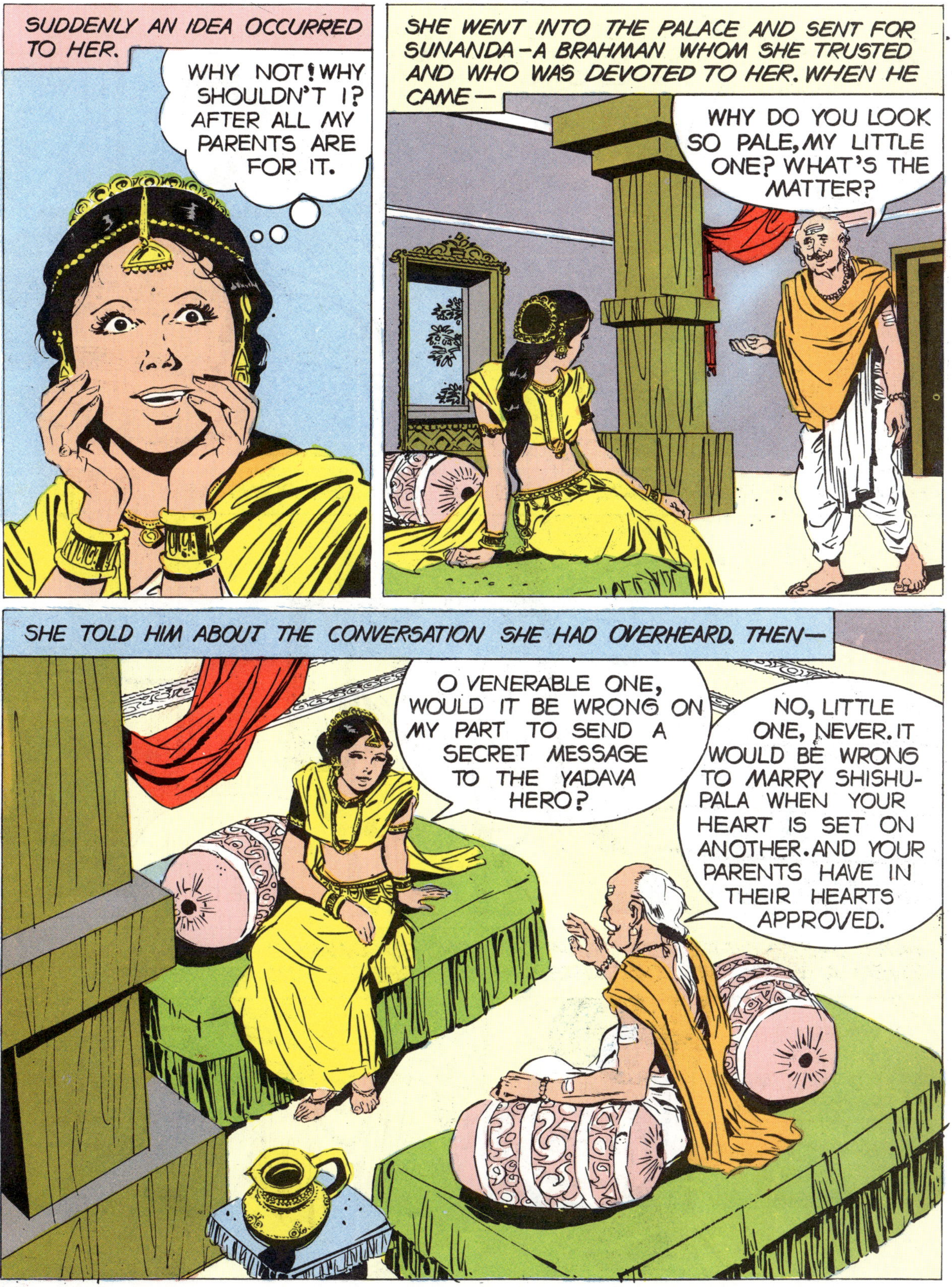

SHE TOLD HIM ABOUT THE CONVERSATION SHE HAD OVERHEARD. THEN—

O VENERABLE ONE, WOULD IT BE WRONG ON MY PART TO SEND A SECRET MESSAGE TO THE YADAVA HERO?

NO, LITTLE ONE, NEVER. IT WOULD BE WRONG TO MARRY SHISHU-PALA WHEN YOUR HEART IS SET ON ANOTHER. AND YOUR PARENTS HAVE IN THEIR HEARTS APPROVED.

BUT WITH WHOM CAN I ENTRUST SUCH A MESSAGE?
I WILL GO TO DWARAKA, RUKMINI. I SHALL CARRY THE MESSAGE FOR YOU.

RUKMINI WROTE OUT THE MESSAGE AND...

... GAVE IT TO THE BRAHMAN, TELLING HIM WHAT HER PLANS WERE.
...AND BE SURE TO TELL HIM THAT I WOULD NOT WANT MY KITH AND KIN TO BE KILLED ON MY ACCOUNT.
DO NOT WORRY, RUKMINI. I WILL NOT FORGET.

WITH GREAT DIFFICULTY, SUNANDA REACHED DWARAKA WHERE HE WAS GIVEN A WARM WELCOME. AFTER HE WAS RESTED AND REFRESHED—
O VENERABLE ONE, IF IT WOULD NOT MEAN BETRAYING ANY CONFIDENCE, TELL US WHY YOU HAVE COME TO OUR INACCESSIBLE CITY?

I HAVE COME WITH A MESSAGE FROM RUKMINI, THE PRINCESS OF VIDARBHA.
RUKMINI! MY OWN RUKMINI!

SUNANDA TOLD KRISHNA ABOUT THE CONVERSATION THAT RUKMINI HAD OVERHEARD. THEN HE GAVE KRISHNA, RUKMINI'S MESSAGE.
...I HAVE CHOSEN YOU AS MY HUSBAND. COME TO VIDARBHA, VANQUISH THE ARMIES OF JARASANDHA AND SHISHUPALA AND CLAIM ME...

WHEN KRISHNA FINISHED READING THE MESSAGE –
IF YOU DO NOT COME AND TAKE HER AWAY SHE HAS DECIDED TO GIVE UP HER LIFE.
SHE MENTIONS THAT IN THE MESSAGE. BUT LITTLE DOES SHE REALISE THAT I TOO HAVE SET MY HEART ON WINNING HER.

* RUKMINI IS BELIEVED TO BE THE GODDESS LAXMI REBORN ON EARTH.

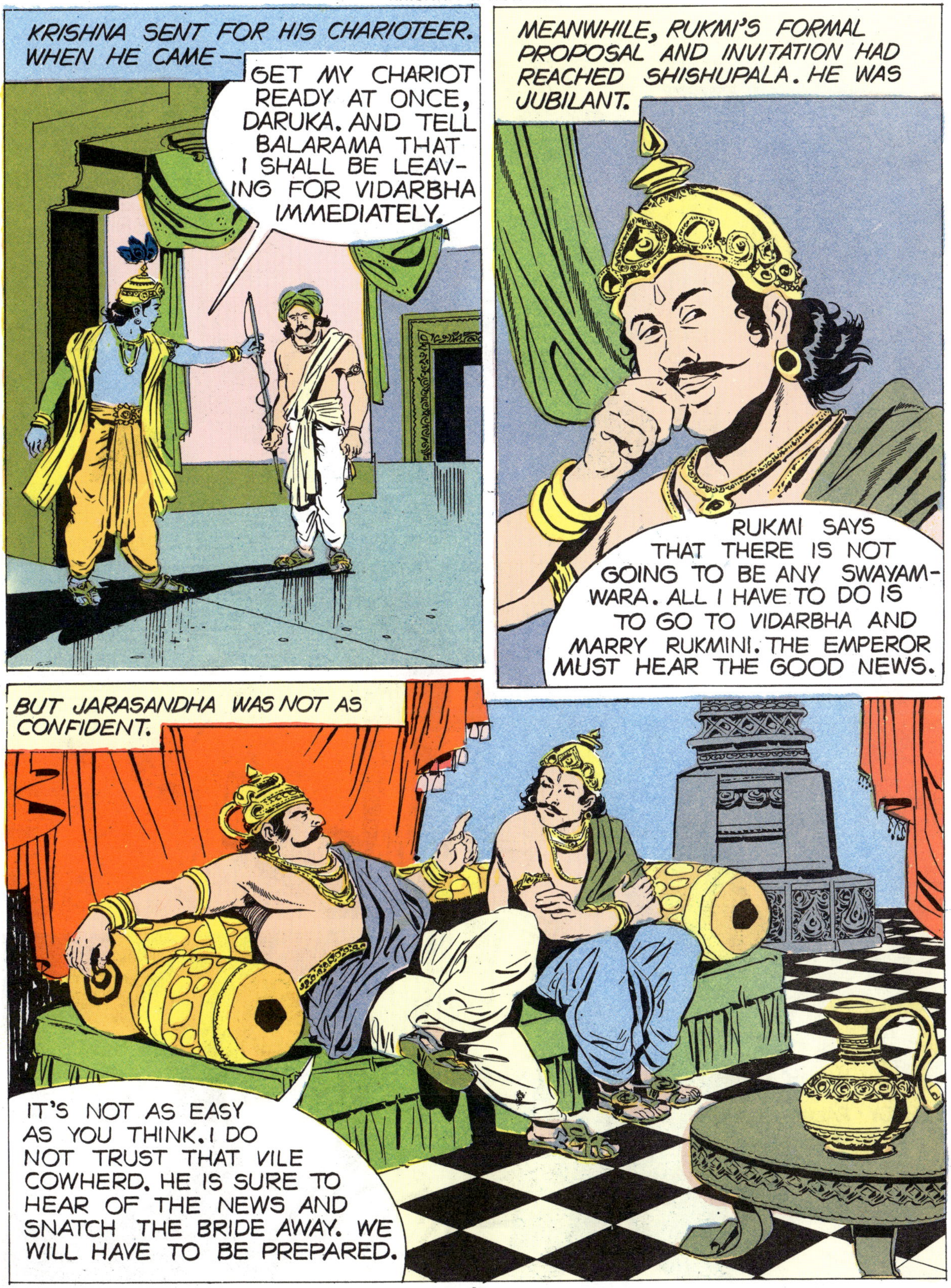

KRISHNA SENT FOR HIS CHARIOTEER. WHEN HE CAME—

GET MY CHARIOT READY AT ONCE, DARUKA. AND TELL BALARAMA THAT I SHALL BE LEAVING FOR VIDARBHA IMMEDIATELY.

MEANWHILE, RUKMI'S FORMAL PROPOSAL AND INVITATION HAD REACHED SHISHUPALA. HE WAS JUBILANT.

RUKMI SAYS THAT THERE IS NOT GOING TO BE ANY SWAYAMWARA. ALL I HAVE TO DO IS TO GO TO VIDARBHA AND MARRY RUKMINI. THE EMPEROR MUST HEAR THE GOOD NEWS.

BUT JARASANDHA WAS NOT AS CONFIDENT.

IT'S NOT AS EASY AS YOU THINK. I DO NOT TRUST THAT VILE COWHERD. HE IS SURE TO HEAR OF THE NEWS AND SNATCH THE BRIDE AWAY. WE WILL HAVE TO BE PREPARED.

JARASANDHA SENT FOR ALL HIS VASSALS AND ALLIES.
I AM BENT ON SECURING THE PRINCESS OF VIDARBHA FOR SHISHUPALA. YOU MUST BE READY TO CONFRONT THE COWHERD IF HE COMES THERE AND TRIES TO TAKE AWAY THE BRIDE.

MEANWHILE, AS SOON AS KRISHNA HAD LEFT DWARAKA, ONE OF BALARAMA'S SPIES CAME TO HIM.
LORD, THE EMPEROR HAS INFORMED ALL HIS ALLIES TO MARCH TO VIDARBHA. HE EXPECTS TROUBLE FROM US.
AND KRISHNA HAS GONE ALL ALONE!
GET MY CHARIOT READY! RALLY OUR ARMIES! ELEPHANTS, HORSES, CHARIOTS, ALL!

AT VIDARBHA, RUKMINI'S ANXIETY, INCREASED WITH EACH PASSING MOMENT.
THE HOUR IS DRAWING NEARER. WHY HAS MY LORD NOT YET COME?

DID MY MESSAGE DISGUST HIM? IF SO, THEN WHY HASN'T SUNANDA RETURNED?

AS SHE LOOKED OUT OF THE WINDOW FOR THE HUNDREDTH TIME, SHE SAW SUNANDA ENTER THE PALACE.
HE LOOKS CHEERFUL. HIS GAIT IS CONFIDENT. HE MUST BRING GOOD NEWS. HIS MISSION HAS BEEN SUCCESSFUL.

SHE TURNED TO HER MAIDS.
YOU MAY GO TO YOUR ROOMS. I WISH TO BE ALONE.

WHEN THEY LEFT, SHE RAN TO THE DOOR OF THE ROOM AND STOOD WAITING FOR THE BRAHMAN.
HE HAS COME, LITTLE ONE. EVERYTHING IS TO GO ACCORDING TO PLAN. HIS BROTHER TOO HAS COME WITH THE YADAVA FORCES.

NEWS OF KRISHNA'S ARRIVAL REACHED BHEESHMAKA, TOO.
KRISHNA HAS ARRIVED. HE HAS COME TO WITNESS THE WEDDING OF THE PRINCESS.
DARE I HOPE THAT HE HAS COME TO CARRY AWAY RUKMINI? DARE I?

HAVE A MANSION READY FOR HIM. FURNISH IT WITH EVERY LUXURY. I SHALL RIDE OUT TO RECEIVE HIM.

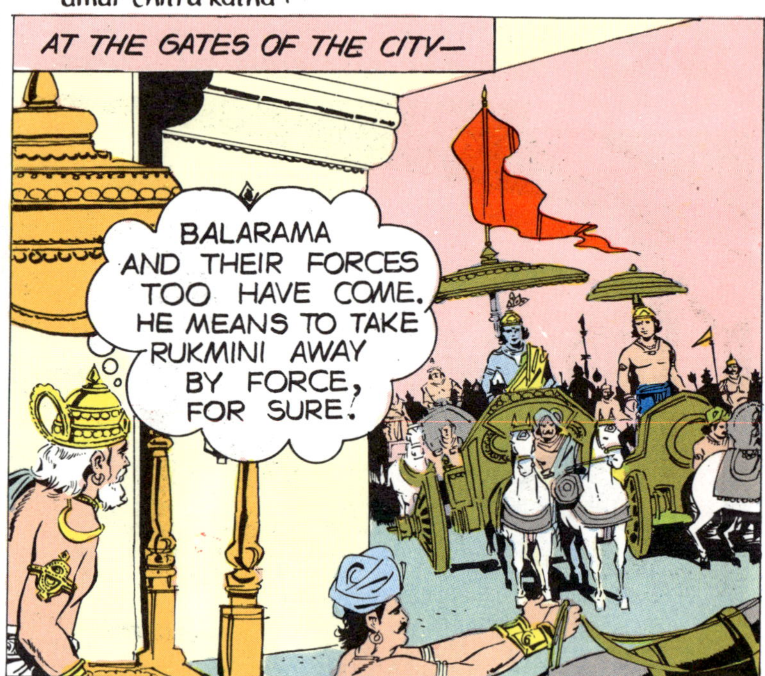
AT THE GATES OF THE CITY—
BALARAMA AND THEIR FORCES TOO HAVE COME. HE MEANS TO TAKE RUKMINI AWAY BY FORCE, FOR SURE!

WELCOME, O PRINCES! WE ARE HAPPY TO SEE YOU HERE. COME LET ME LEAD YOU TO THE PALACE WHERE YOU WILL STAY.

AS THEY RODE INTO THE CITY, THEY PASSED THE SHRINE OF GODDESS PARVATI, THE FAMILY DEITY OF THE ROYAL HOUSEHOLD.
AH! THAT IS THE TEMRLE RUKMINI WROTE ABOUT. HOW ANXIOUS MY DEAR ONE MUST BE.

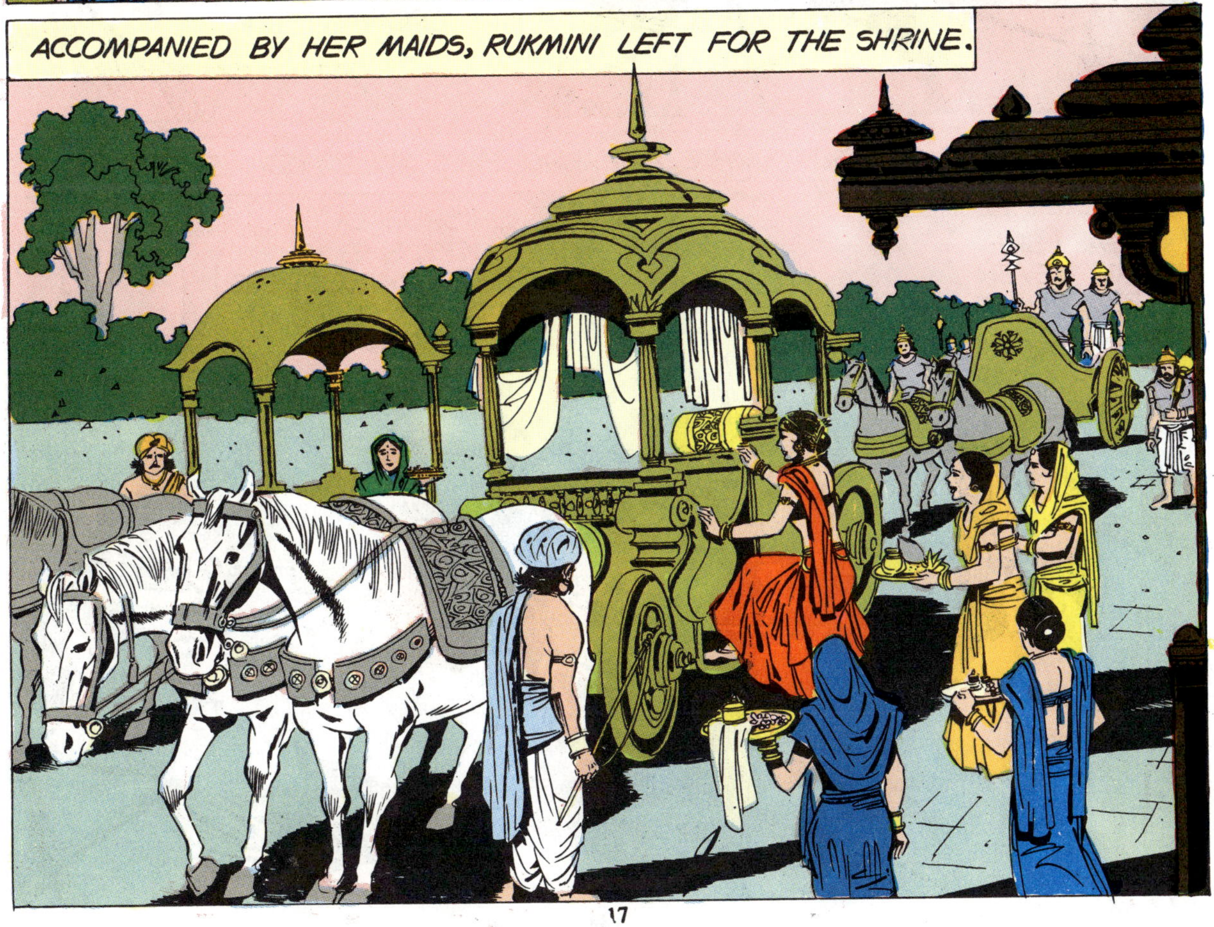

ACCOMPANIED BY HER MAIDS, RUKMINI LEFT FOR THE SHRINE.

WHEN THEY REACHED THE GATES OF THE TEMPLE COURTYARD, SHE STEPPED OUT OF HER CHARIOT.

I DO NOT SEE KRISHNA AMONG THEM. THEY SAY HE IS DARK, WEARS A YELLOW ROBE, AND SPORTS A PEACOCK FEATHER IN HIS CROWN.

AS SHE WALKED TO THE TEMPLE, A MYRIAD EYES FOLLOWED HER EVERY MOVEMENT, DRINKING IN HER BEAUTY.

ALAS! SHE CAN NEVER BE MINE.

SHISHUPALA IS LUCKY. SHE IS THE VERY GODDESS OF WEALTH* INCARNATE.

* LAXMI

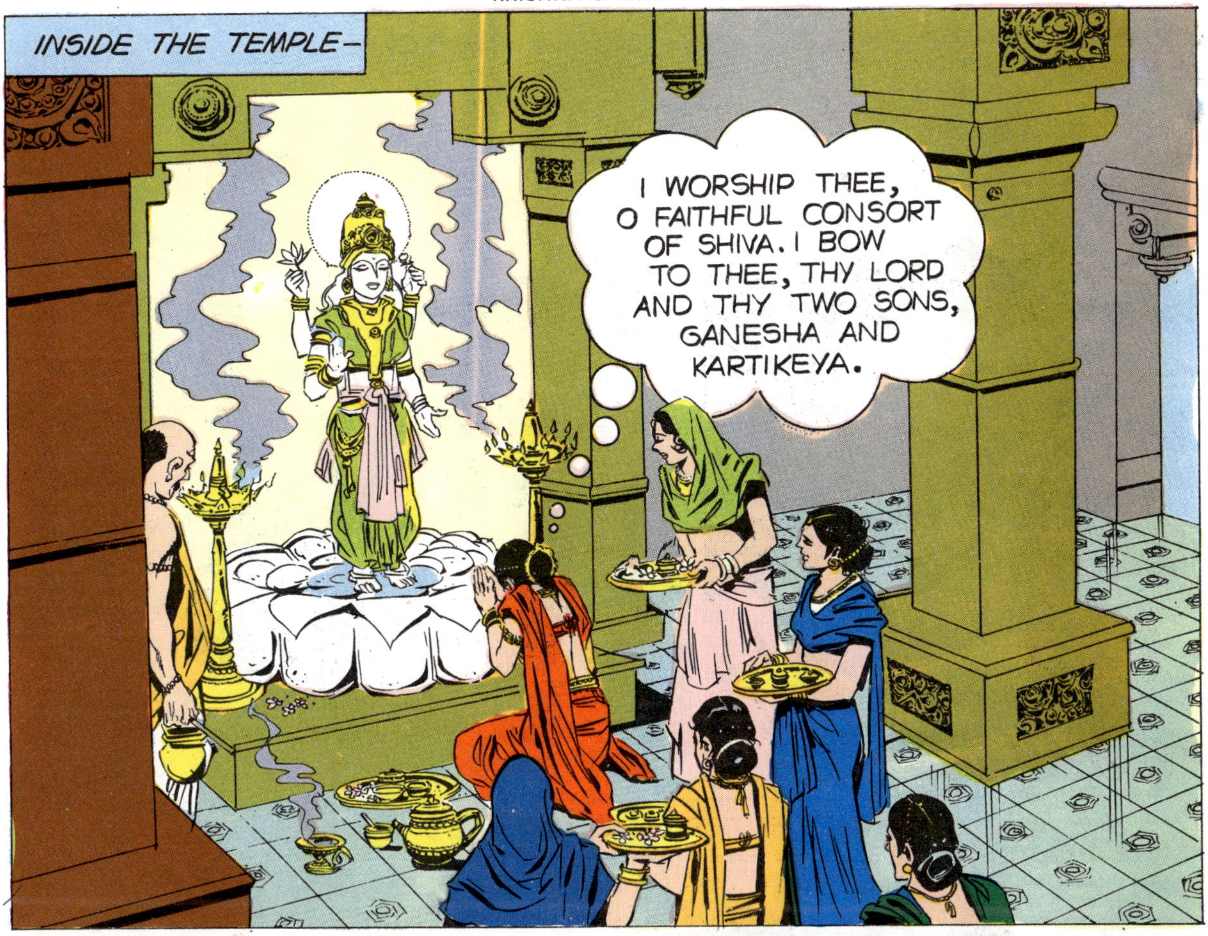

INSIDE THE TEMPLE—

I WORSHIP THEE, O FAITHFUL CONSORT OF SHIVA. I BOW TO THEE, THY LORD AND THY TWO SONS, GANESHA AND KARTIKEYA.

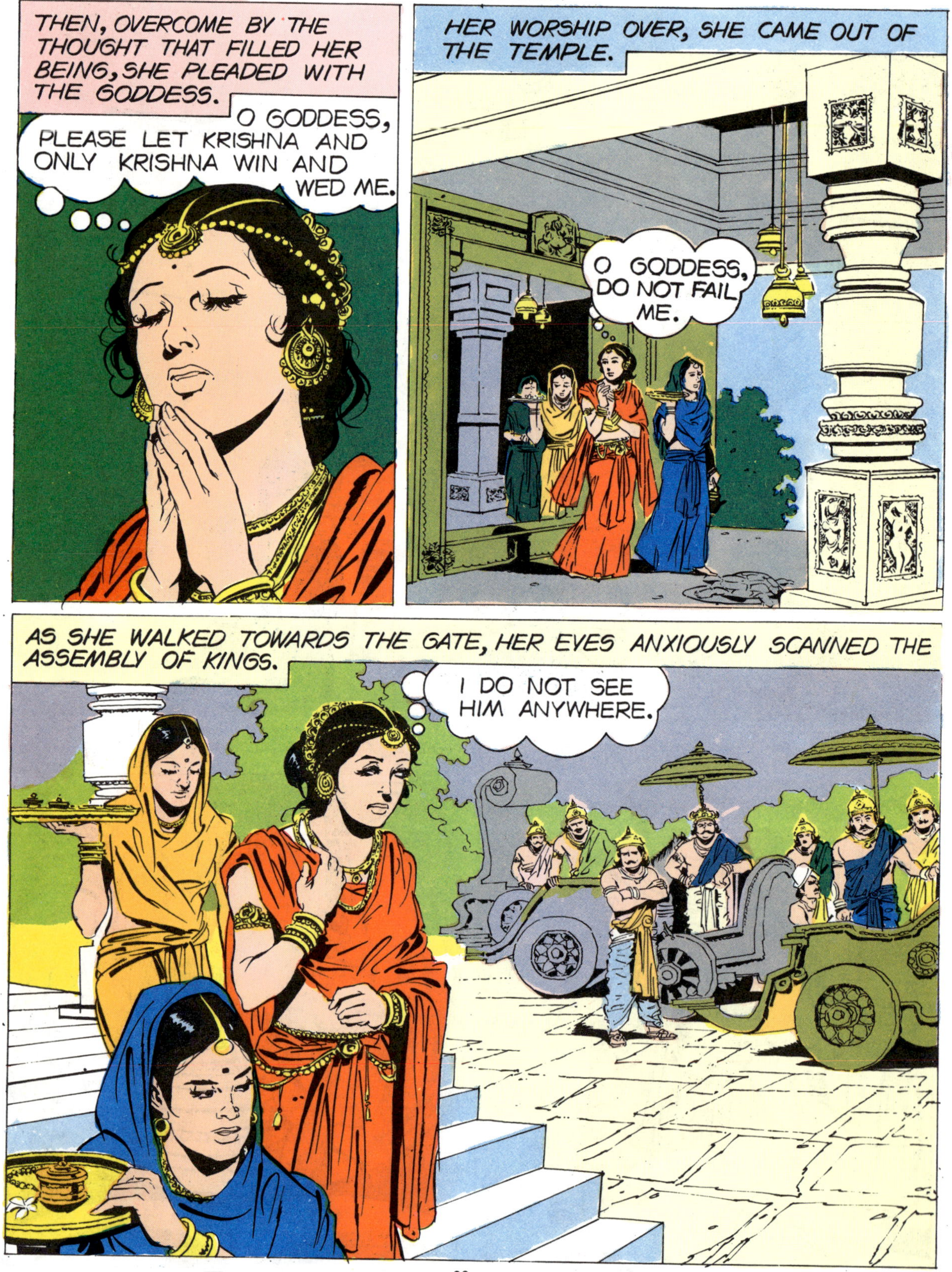

AS SHE WALKED TOWARDS THE GATE, HER EYES ANXIOUSLY SCANNED THE ASSEMBLY OF KINGS.

I DO NOT SEE HIM ANYWHERE.

HEAVY WAS HER HEART AND SLOW HER GAIT. THE CHARIOT LOOMED BEFORE HER ALL TOO SOON.
WILL KRISHNA EVER BECOME...

...MINE?

RUKMINI. IT'S ME. YOUR KRISHNA.

AND THE NEXT MOMENT SHE WAS SEATED NEXT TO HIM IN HIS CHARIOT.
STOP HIM!
RUKMINI! WAIT!

BUT KRISHNA'S CHARIOT SPED AWAY BLOWING DUST INTO THE EYES OF THE BEMUSED KINGS.

JARASANDHA WAS FURIOUS.
WHERE IS YOUR KSHATRIYA VALOUR? WHY DO YOU STAND THERE, AS IF YOU'VE LOST YOUR SENSES. PURSUE THEM!

JERKED INTO ACTION, THE KINGS CHARGED FORWARD.

BALARAMA TURNED TO KRISHNA.
THEY'RE GIVING CHASE. YOU RIDE ON. WE'LL FALL BACK AND DEAL WITH THEM.

WHILE BALARAMA WAS BUSY TACKLING JARASANDHA, SHISHUPALA AND THEIR HORDES, RUKMI CHARGED AHEAD AFTER KRISHNA'S VANISHING CHARIOT.

BALARAMA DID NOT TRY TO STOP HIM.

BALARAMA'S ONSLAUGHT WAS FIERCE.
LET US RETREAT, SHISHUPALA. THERE IS NO HOPE LEFT. THE COWHERDS ARE DETERMINED. RUKMINI IS LOST TO YOU.
ALAS! I FEEL AS IF MY WEDDED WIFE HAS BEEN ABDUCTED. SO SURE WAS I THAT SHE WAS MINE ALONE.

JARASANDHA TRIED TO CONSOLE HIM.
DON'T GRIEVE, SHISHUPALA. FORTUNE FAVOURED THEM AND THEY WON. WE SHALL CERTAINLY DEFEAT THEM WHEN OUR LUCK TURNS.

FULL OF HATRED FOR THE MAN WHO HAD WORSTED THEM, THE DISAPPOINTED SUITOR AND HIS WELL-WISHERS RETURNED TO THEIR CAPITALS.

MEANWHILE, RUKMI HAD ALMOST CAUGHT UP WITH KRISHNA.
TODAY I SHALL HUMBLE THE PRIDE OF THAT COWHERD WHO DARED ABDUCT MY SISTER.

FASTER...
FASTER...
FASTER...

SOON HIS CHARIOT WAS BUT A FEW FEET AWAY FROM KRISHNA.
STOP! STOP! WAIT, YOU–DISGRACE TO THE RACE OF YADU! HOW DARE YOU KIDNAP MY SISTER, EVEN AS A CROW STEALS A SACRED OFFERING!

YOU WILY RASCAL. YOU HAVE PROVED YOUR CUNNING, NOW PROVE YOUR VALOUR.

RUKMI'S ARROW DID NOT EVEN MAKE A DENT IN KRISHNA'S ARMOUR.

KRISHNA PULLED OUT AN ARROW AND...

...LIFTED HIS BOW.

HE FIRST KILLED RUKMI'S HORSES AND...

...THEN SHATTERED HIS CHARIOT.

RUKMI TOOK COVER
BEHIND THE DEBRIS...

...AND LIFTED HIS BOW...

...ONLY TO HAVE IT BROKEN
TO BITS.

MAD WITH RAGE, RUKMI PICKED
UP HIS SWORD...

...AND RUSHED TOWARDS KRISHNA.

THE NEXT MOMENT, HOWEVER FOUND HIM HOLDING BUT THE HILT.

AS HE THREW IT AWAY IN DISGUST, KRISHNA PICKED UP HIS SWORD AND...

...WAS ABOUT TO RUSH TOWARDS HIM WHEN—
O VIRTUOUS LORD, PLEASE SPARE MY BROTHER. PLEASE DON'T KILL HIM.
ARISE, RUKMINI. FOR YOUR SAKE, RUKMI SHALL LIVE.

HE WENT UP TO RUKMI AND BOUND HIM WITH HIS OWN PRAPATA.*
I SHALL SHAVE OFF HALF HIS HAIR AND HALF HIS MOUSTACHE WITH THE BLADE OF MY SWORD. THERE COULD BE NO GREATER PUNISHMENT FOR A WARRIOR.

BALARAMA WAS HORRIFIED.
KRISHNA! WHAT ARE YOU DOING?

* CUMMERBUND.

KRISHNA, YOU HAVE PERFORMED AN IMPIOUS ACT; AN ACT DETESTED BY OUR RACE. TO DO WHAT YOU HAVE DONE TO A RELATIVE IS WORSE THAN KILLING HIM.

THEN HE TURNED TO RUKMINI.
PLEASE DO NOT TAKE OFFENCE, DEAR SISTER. YOUR BROTHER UNFORTUNATELY HAS REAPED THE FRUIT OF HIS OWN ACTIONS.

YOU ARE FREE TO GO, RUKMI.
ALAS! HE HAS ONLY ADDED INSULT TO INJURY. IT WERE BETTER THAT THEY HAD KILLED ME.

AS THE HUMILIATED RUKMI SLOWLY WALKED AWAY—

BUT WHERE SHALL I GO? BOUND BY MY OWN VOW, I CANNOT RETURN TO MY CAPITAL. I WILL HAVE TO BUILD A NEW CITY FOR MYSELF.